RESURRECTION SUNDAY

Written by Robin Loisch
Illustrated by Michael Denman

Long ago, God sent His Son, Jesus, to the world to offer us a special gift.

What does the Bible say? Use the code to find out.

___ ___ ___ ___ ___ ___ ___ ___ ___ ___ ___ ___ ___
23 19   2   17 19   6 19 11 24   2   10   4 24

___ ___ ___ ___ ___ ___ ___ ___ ___ ___ ___ ___ ___ ___ ___
15 19   9   6   2   10   4 26 10   4 24   23 26 11 24

___ ___ ___ ___ ___ ___ ___ ___ ___ ___ ___ ___ ___
 4 22 17   19   7 24   26   7   2   19   7   6 14

___ ___ ___, ___ ___ ___ ___ ___ ___ ___ ___ ___ ___ ___
17 19   7   10   4 26 10   15   4 19 24 11 24   9

___ ___ ___ ___ ___ ___ ___ ___ ___ ___ ___ ___ ___
 1 24   6 22 24 11 24 17   22   7   4 22 20

___ ___ ___ ___ ___ ___ ___ ___ ___ ___ ___ ___ ___ ___
17   4 26   6   6   7 19 10   8 24   9 22 17   4

___ ___ ___ ___ ___ ___ ___ ___ ___ ___ ___ ___ ___ ___
 1 16 10   4 26 11 24   24 10 24   9   7 26   6

___ ___ ___ ___. ___ ___ ___ ___ ___ 3:16 (NIV)
 6 22   3 24   5 19   4   7

A=26	B=1	C=25	D=2
E=24	F=3	G=23	H=4
I=22	J=5	K=21	L=6
M=20	N=7	O=19	P=8
Q=18	R=9	S=17	T=10
U=16	V=11	W=15	X=12
Y=14	Z=13		

When Jesus was a boy, He went to the temple.
The teachers were surprised at how much He knew about God.
Jesus knew God had a special job for Him to do when He grew up.

Help Mary, Joseph, and Jesus find the temple.

3

Jesus wanted to be baptized before He began His work.
When Jesus came up from the water, God sent down His spirit.

What did God say? Unscramble the words.
Then use the circled letters to answer the question.

(STIH) __ __ __ __   IS MY

(ONS) __ __ __ ,   (MOHW) __ __ __ __   I

(VEOL) __ __ __ __ ;   WITH HIM I AM WELL

(APELSDE) __ __ __ __ __ __ __ .

Matthew 3:17 (NIV)

What did God's Spirit look like?

__ __ __ __ __

Jesus chose 12 men to help with His work. Then He began teaching people about God. Jesus also healed sick people and did many other miracles.

What is another name for the group of men Jesus chose?
Write the first letter of each picture in the box to find out.

5

At last, the time came for Jesus to go to Jerusalem for the Passover celebration. Jesus told the disciples to bring an animal for him to ride.

What was it? Connect the dots to find out.

6

The people put their coats on the ground for Jesus to ride on.
They waved palm branches. The leaders of the city became very angry
when they saw how the people loved Jesus.

What did the people shout? Use the code to find out.

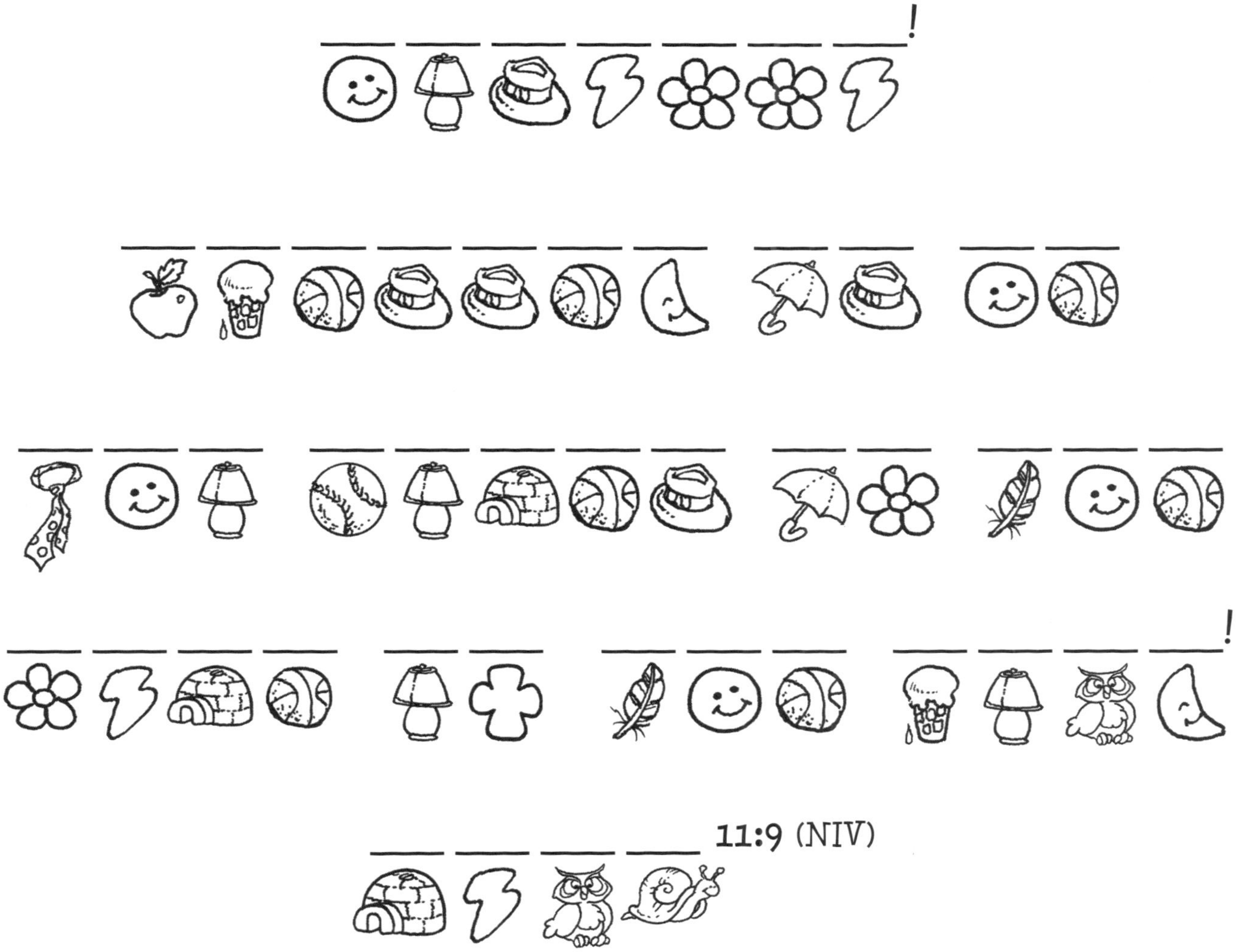

___ ___ ___ ___ ___ ___ ___!

___ ___ ___ ___ ___ ___ ___   ___ ___   ___ ___

___ ___ ___ ___ ___ ___ ___ ___ ___   ___ ___ ___   ___ ___

___ ___ ___ ___ ___ ___   ___ ___ ___   ___ ___ ___ ___!

___ ___ ___ ___ 11:9 (NIV)

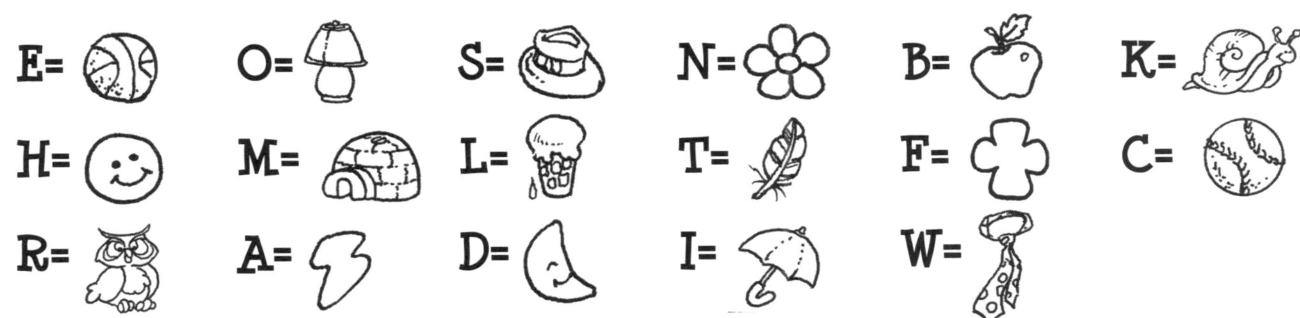

E=   O=   S=   N=   B=   K=

H=   M=   L=   T=   F=   C=

R=   A=   D=   I=   W=

Jesus and His disciples were eating the Passover meal.
During their time together, Jesus washed His disciples' feet.
He wanted to teach them to serve others.

What did Jesus say? Write the letters from the puzzle pieces
in the matching pieces in the grid to find out.

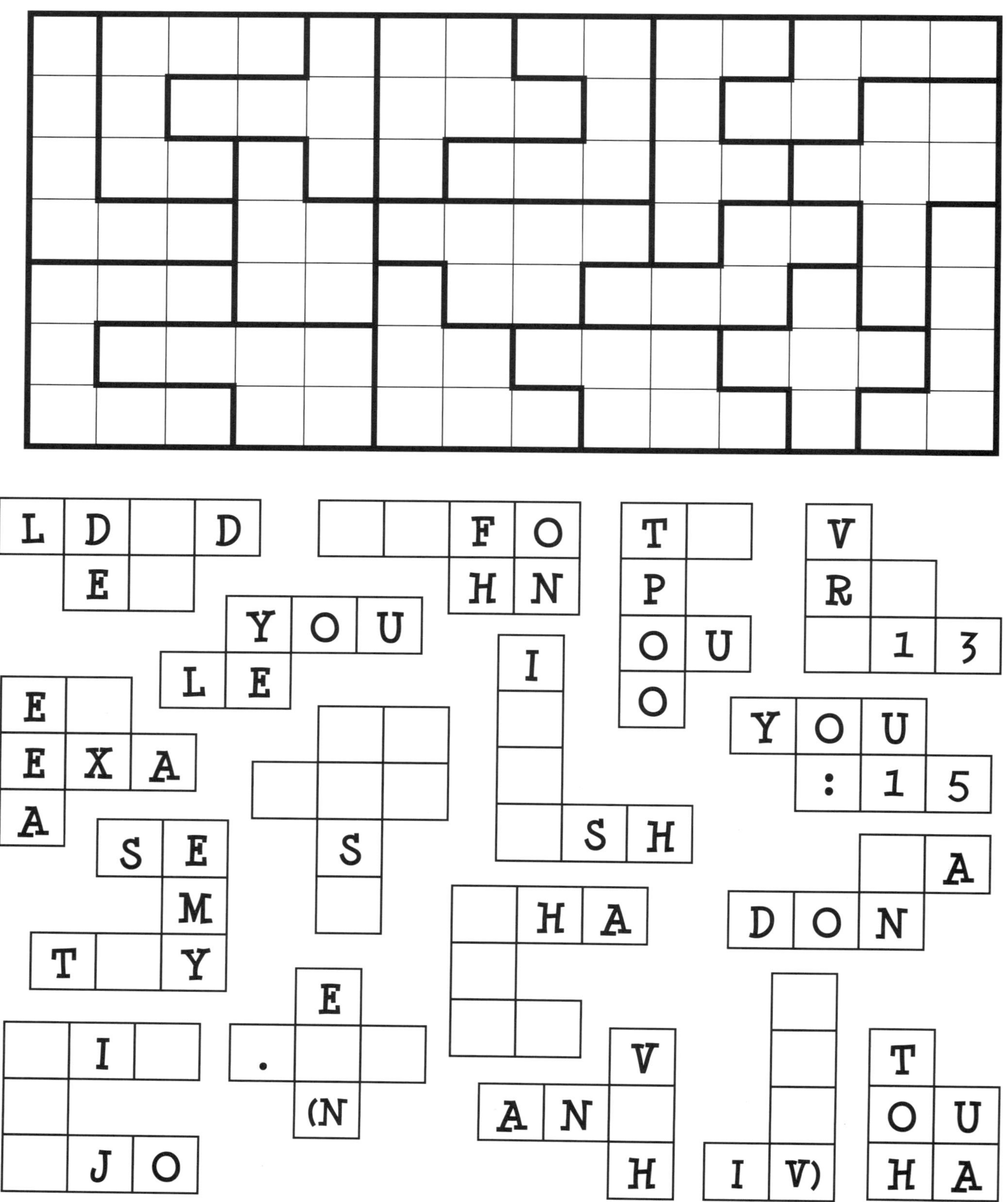

While they ate, Jesus told His disciples many things.
As He shared bread and wine with them, Jesus told them He was giving up
His body and blood. What else did Jesus say?

Cross out every Q. Then write the letters you have left in order
on the line to read the answer.

——— ——— ——— ——— ——— ——— ——— ——— ——— ——— ——— ——— ——— ———

——— ——— ——— ——— ——— ——— ——— ——— ——— ——— ——— ——— ——— ———

——— ——— ———   ——— ———. Luke 22:19 (NIV)

While Jesus was praying in the garden, Judas brought men with swords to capture Jesus. The disciples were scared and ran away.

Help the disciples find their way out of the garden.

Jesus was taken before Pilate to be judged. Pilate knew Jesus had done
nothing wrong, but the crowd shouted terrible words.
Soldiers took Jesus away and put a crown of thorns on His head.

What did the crowd shout? Find 10 hidden letters.
Unscramble them to read the words.

____ ______ ____!

Matthew 27:22 (NIV)

11

At Golgotha, Jesus was nailed to a cross where He died.
Because Jesus gave the gift of His life, we can be forgiven of our sins
and can go to heaven someday.

What does Golgotha mean?

Go down the first row on the grid. When you come to a shaded box,
write that letter on the line below the puzzle. Continue to the last row.
Then separate the letters into words to read the Bible verse.

Luke 23:33 (NIV)

Joseph of Arimathea took Jesus' body and put it in a new tomb.
Then a huge stone was rolled in front of the door.

Circle the hidden pictures:
dove, lily, Bible, cross, perfume bottle, grapes, cup, turtle

Three days after Jesus' death, two of His friends came to the tomb.
The stone was rolled away!
They saw an angel and ran to tell the disciples what he said.

What did the angel say? Write the letter that comes BEFORE the letter
under the lines to find out.

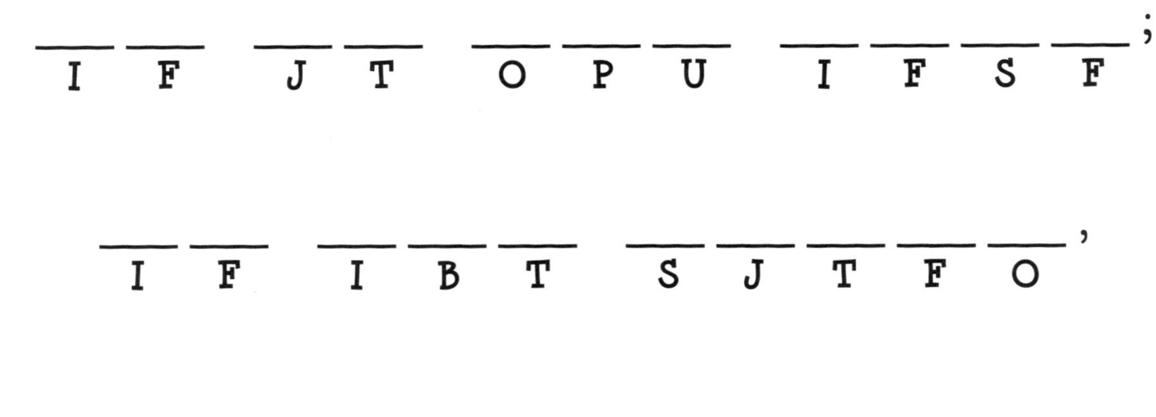

__ __ __ __ __ __ __ __ __ __ __ ;
I F   J T   O P U   I F S F

__ __ __ __ __ __ __ __ __ __ ,
I F   I B T   S J T F O

__ __ __ __ __ __ __ __ __ __ __ .
K V T U   B T   I F   T B J E

__ __ __ __ __ __ __ 28:6 (NIV)
N B U U I F X

Crossword Puzzle

Use the clues to fill in the crossword puzzle.
Hint: Look up the Bible verses if you need help.

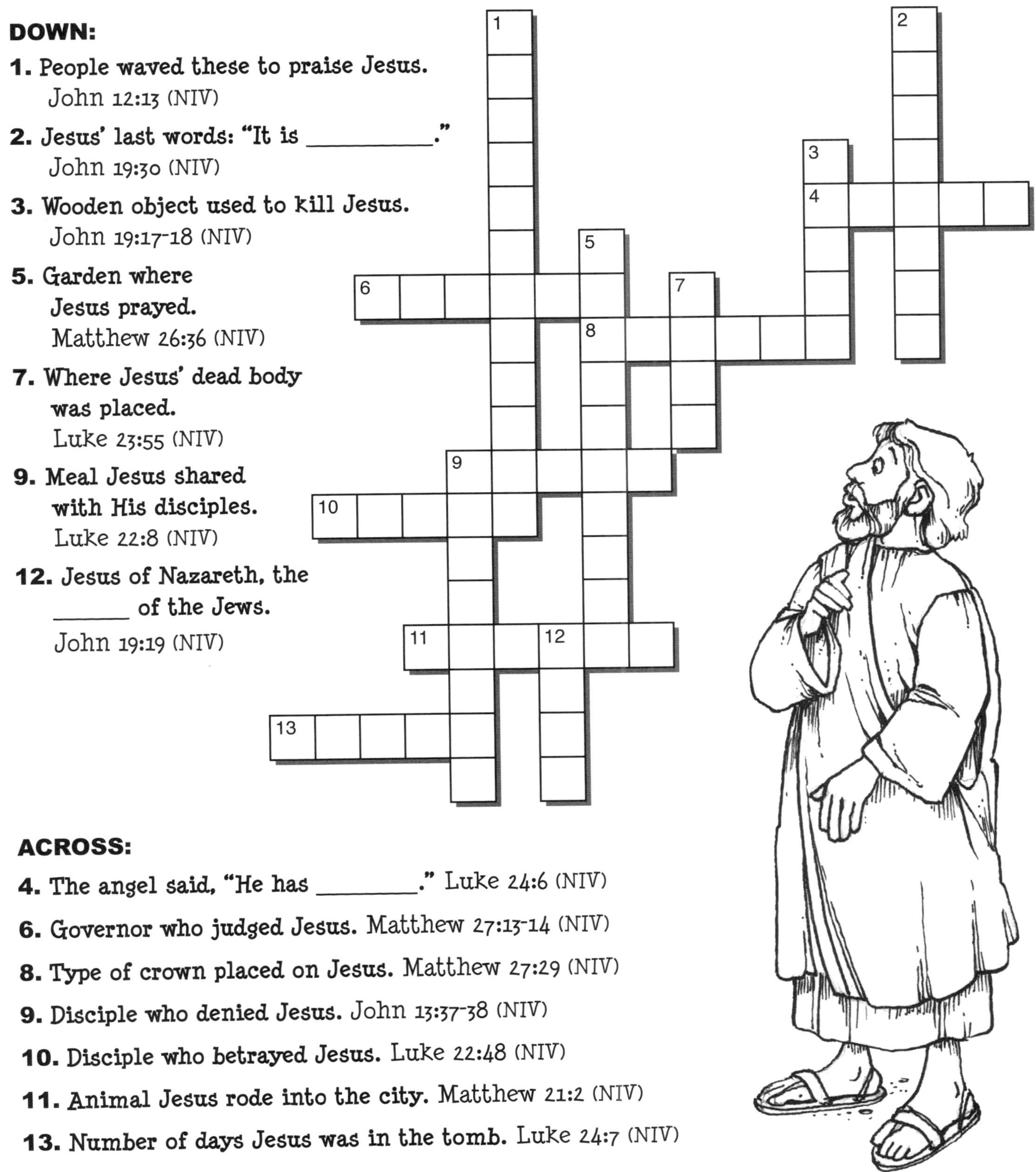

DOWN:

1. People waved these to praise Jesus.
John 12:13 (NIV)

2. Jesus' last words: "It is __________."
John 19:30 (NIV)

3. Wooden object used to kill Jesus.
John 19:17-18 (NIV)

5. Garden where
Jesus prayed.
Matthew 26:36 (NIV)

7. Where Jesus' dead body
was placed.
Luke 23:55 (NIV)

9. Meal Jesus shared
with His disciples.
Luke 22:8 (NIV)

12. Jesus of Nazareth, the
_______ of the Jews.
John 19:19 (NIV)

ACROSS:

4. The angel said, "He has ________." Luke 24:6 (NIV)

6. Governor who judged Jesus. Matthew 27:13-14 (NIV)

8. Type of crown placed on Jesus. Matthew 27:29 (NIV)

9. Disciple who denied Jesus. John 13:37-38 (NIV)

10. Disciple who betrayed Jesus. Luke 22:48 (NIV)

11. Animal Jesus rode into the city. Matthew 21:2 (NIV)

13. Number of days Jesus was in the tomb. Luke 24:7 (NIV)

Answer Key

PAGE 2

God so loved the world that he gave his one and only Son, that whoever believes in him shall not perish but have eternal life. John 3:16 (NIV)

PAGE 3

PAGE 4

This is my Son, whom I love; with him I am well pleased.
DOVE

PAGE 5

The disciples

PAGE 7

Hosanna! Blessed is he who comes in the name of the Lord! Mark 11:9 (NIV)

PAGE 8

I		H	A	V	E		S	E	T		Y	O	U
		A	N		E	X	A	M	P	L	E		
			T	H	A	T		Y	O	U			
	S	H	O	U	L	D		D	O		A	S	
	I		H	A	V	E		D	O	N	E		
		F	O	R		Y	O	U	.				
	J	O	H	N		1	3	:	1	5	(N	I	V)

PAGE 9

Do this in remembrance of me.

PAGE 10

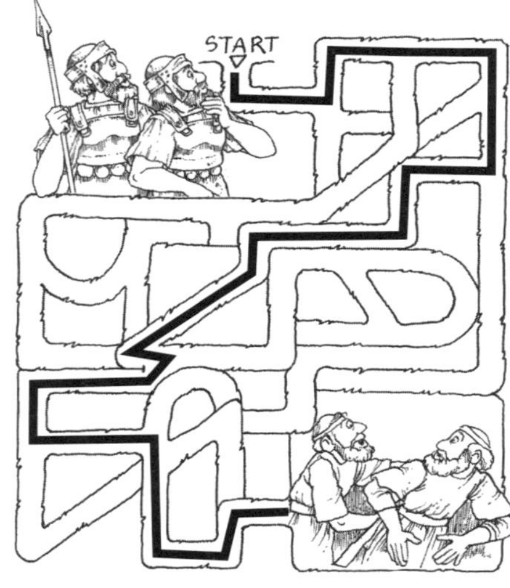

PAGE 11

Crucify Him

PAGE 12

The place called the Skull.

PAGE 13

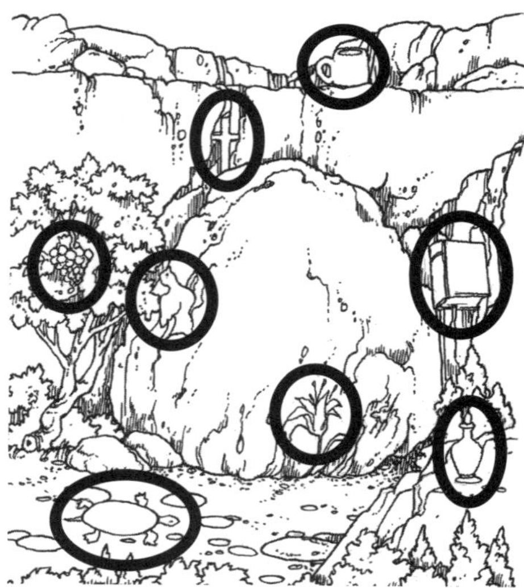

PAGE 14

He is not here; he has risen, just as he said.
Matthew 28:6 (NIV)

PAGE 15